Adapted Reading and Stud...

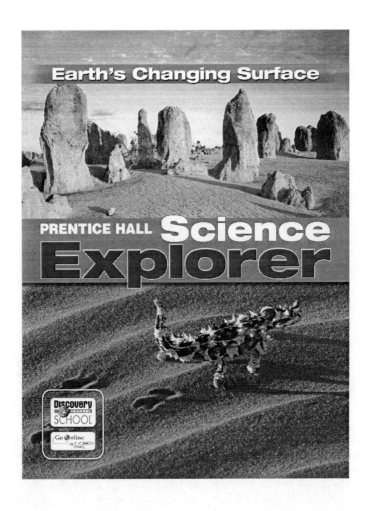

Boston, Massachusetts
Upper Saddle River, New Jersey

Copyright © by Pearson Education, Inc., publishing as Pearson Prentice Hall, Boston, Massachusetts 02116. All rights reserved. Printed in the United States of America. This publication is protected by copyright, and permission should be obtained from the publisher prior to any prohibited reproduction, storage in a retrieval system, or transmission in any form or by any means, electronic, mechanical, photocopying, recording, or likewise. The publisher hereby grants permission to reproduce these pages, in part or in whole, for classroom use only, the number not to exceed the number of students in each class. Notice of copyright must appear on all copies. For information regarding permission(s), write to: Rights and Permissions Department, One Lake Street, Upper Saddle River, New Jersey 07458.

Pearson Prentice Hall™ is a trademark of Pearson Education, Inc.
Pearson® is a registered trademark of Pearson plc.
Prentice Hall® is a registered trademark of Pearson Education, Inc.

ISBN 0-13-166545-6
9 10 V036 15 14 13 12 11 10

Earth's Changing Surface

Chapter 1 Mapping Earth's Surface
1 Exploring Earth's Surface 4
2 Models of Earth 7
3 Maps and Computers 13
4 Topographic Maps 15

Chapter 2 Weathering and Soil Formation
1 Rocks and Weathering 18
2 How Soil Forms 23
3 Soil Conservation 28

Chapter 3 Erosion and Deposition
1 Changing Earth's Surface 31
2 Water Erosion 34
3 The Force of Moving Water 39
4 Glaciers 42
5 Waves 45
6 Wind 48

Chapter 4 A Trip Through Geologic Time
1 Fossils 50
2 The Relative Age of Rocks 53
3 Radioactive Dating 56
4 The Geologic Time Scale 59
5 Early Earth 62
6 Eras of Earth's History 65

Name _____ Date _____ Class _____

Mapping Earth's Surface

Exploring Earth's Surface (pages 6–10)

Topography (page 7)

Key Concept: **The topography of an area includes the area's elevation, relief, and landforms.**

- **Topography** (tuh PAWG ruh fee) is the shape of the land. An area's topography may be flat, sloping, hilly, or mountainous.
- **Elevation** is a place's height above sea level. Mountains have high elevation. Valleys have low elevation.
- **Relief** is the difference in elevation between the highest points and lowest points of an area. An area with mountains and valleys has high relief.
- A **landform** is a feature of the land such as a hill or valley.

Answer the following question. Use your textbook and the ideas above.

1. Read the words in the box. In each sentence below, fill in one of the words.

relief   topography   elevation   landform

   a. A place's height above sea level is its _____.

   b. A feature of the land such as a valley is a(an) _____.

   c. The difference in elevation between the highest and lowest points of an area is the area's _____.

Mapping Earth's Surface

Types of Landforms (pages 8–10)

Key Concept: **There are three main types of landforms: plains, mountains, and plateaus.**

- A **plain** is a landform with nearly flat or gently rolling land. A plain has low relief.
- A **mountain** is a landform with peaks and steep sides. A mountain has high elevation and high relief.
- A **mountain range** is a group of mountains in the same area. The mountains in a range formed around the same time.
- A mountain system is a group of mountain ranges in the same region. The Rocky Mountains are an example of a mountain system.
- A **plateau** is a landform with high elevation and a flat surface.
- A **landform region** is a large area where there is mainly just one type of landform. The Great Plains is a landform region. The Great Plains is an area of plains that covers several states.

Answer the following questions. Use your textbook and the ideas above.

2. Draw a line from each term to its meaning.

Term	Meaning
mountain	a. landform with nearly flat or gently rolling land
plain	b. landform with high elevation and a flat surface
plateau	c. landform with high elevation and high relief

Name _____ Date _____ Class _____

Mapping Earth's Surface

3. Fill in the blanks in the concept map about landforms.

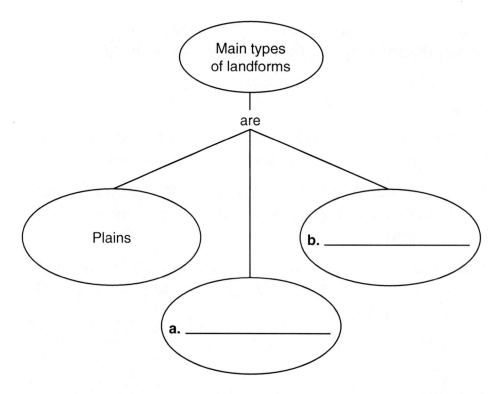

4. Fill in the blanks in the table about mountain landforms.

Mountain Landforms	
Kind of Mountain Landform	**Description**
a. _____	landform with peaks and steep sides
Mountain range	group of mountains
b. _____	group of mountain ranges

Name _____ Date _____ Class _____

Mapping Earth's Surface

Models of Earth (pages 11–19)

Maps and Globes (page 12)

Key Concept: **Maps and globes are drawn to scale and use symbols to represent topography and other features on Earth's surface.**

- A **map** is a flat model of all or part of Earth's surface. A map shows the surface as it looks from above.
- A **globe** is a sphere that models all of Earth's surface. A globe shows Earth as it looks from space.
- The **scale** of a map shows how distance on the map compares to distance on the surface. For example, one centimeter on a map might be the same as one kilometer on the surface.
- **Symbols** on a map stand for features such as rivers, highways, or cities. The **key** of a map shows what the symbols stand for.
- A compass rose or north arrow shows how directions on a map compare to directions on the surface. The top of a map usually is north.

Answer the following questions. Use your textbook and the ideas above.

1. A flat model of Earth's surface is a(an)

    _____.

2. Circle the letter of each sentence that is true about globes.
    a. Globes are spheres.
    b. Globes model all of Earth's surface.
    c. Globes show Earth as it looks from space.

Name _____ Date _____ Class _____

Mapping Earth's Surface

3. Read the words in the box. In each sentence below, fill in one of the words.

| scale   compass   key   symbol |

   a. A feature such as a city is shown on a map with a _____.

   b. Distance on a map is compared to distance on the surface by the map's _____.

   c. You can see how roads are shown on a map by looking at the map's _____.

An Earth Reference System (pages 13–15)

Key Concept: Most maps and globes show a grid of lines on Earth's surface. Two of the lines that make up the grid, the equator and prime meridian, are the baselines for measuring distances on Earth's surface.

- Earth is a sphere. Distances around a sphere are measured in **degrees** (°). The distance all the way around a sphere is 360°.

- The **equator** is an imaginary line that goes around Earth halfway between the North Pole and the South Pole.

- The equator divides Earth into two halves. The two halves are called the Northern Hemisphere and Southern Hemisphere. A **hemisphere** (HEM ih sfeer) is one half of Earth's surface.

- The **prime meridian** is an imaginary line that goes through the North Pole and the South Pole. The prime meridian passes through Greenwich, England.

Name _____ Date _____ Class _____

Mapping Earth's Surface

- Another imaginary line through both poles lies opposite the prime meridian. That line and the prime meridian divide Earth into two halves. The two halves are called the Eastern Hemisphere and Western Hemisphere.

Answer the following question. Use your textbook and the ideas on page 8 and above.

4. Fill in the blanks in the drawing of Earth's surface.

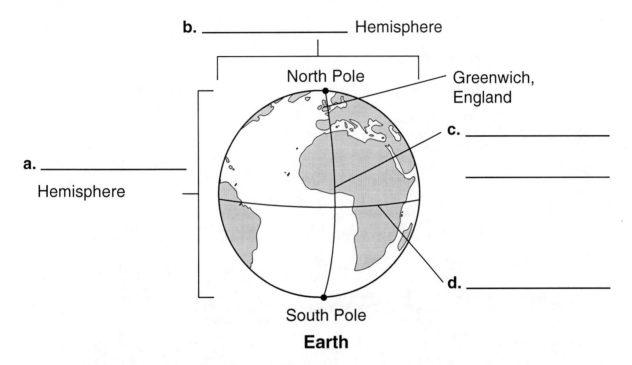

Locating Points on Earth's Surface (pages 16–17)

Key Concept: **The lines of latitude and longitude form a grid that can be used to find locations anywhere on Earth.**

- **Latitude** is distance north or south of the equator. Lines of latitude go around the globe from east to west. All lines of latitude are parallel to the equator.

- The latitude of the equator is 0°. The latitude of the North Pole is 90° North. The latitude of the South Pole is 90° South.

Name _____ Date _____ Class _____

Mapping Earth's Surface

- **Longitude** is distance east or west of the prime meridian. Lines of longitude go around the globe from north to south. All lines of longitude pass through both poles.

- The longitude of the prime meridian is 0°. Longitude goes up to 180° East and 180° West.

- You can find any place on a map or globe if you know the place's latitude and longitude.

Answer the following question. Use your textbook and the ideas on page 9 and above.

5. Use the map below to answer the following questions.

   a. What is the latitude of New Orleans, Louisiana? _____

   b. What is the longitude of New Orleans, Louisiana? _____

   c. What city on the map has latitude of 30° North and longitude of 120° East? _____

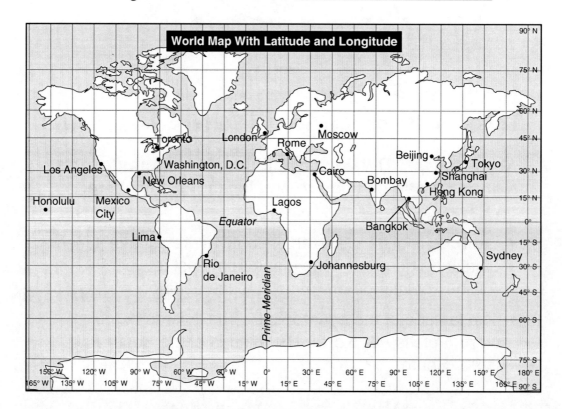

Name _____ Date _____ Class _____

Mapping Earth's Surface

Map Projections (pages 18–19)

Key Concept: **Three common map projections are the Mercator projection, the equal-area projection, and the conic projection.**

- A **map projection** is a way to show Earth's curved surface on a flat map.

- A Mercator projection has straight lines of latitude and straight lines of longitude. The lines form a grid of rectangles. This kind of map spreads out lands near the poles, so these lands look bigger than they really are.

- An equal-area projection has straight lines of latitude and curved lines of longitude. All the lines of longitude pass through the North and South Poles. This kind of map spreads out lands near the edges of the map.

- A conic projection has curved lines of latitude and straight lines of longitude. This kind of map makes lands the right size and shape, but only for small areas of the surface.

Answer the following questions. Use your textbook and the ideas above.

6. Draw a line from each kind of map projection to the correct description.

Kind of Map Projection	Description
equal-area projection	a. makes lands near the poles look bigger
Mercator projection	b. makes a region such as a continent look the right size and shape
conic projection	c. makes lands near the edges look stretched out

Name _____ Date _____ Class _____

Mapping Earth's Surface

7. Label each map with the kind of projection it shows.

a. _____
_____

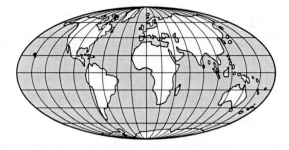

b. _____
_____

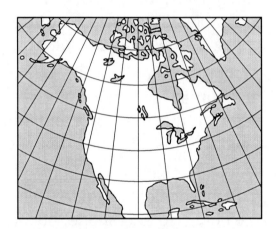

c. _____
_____

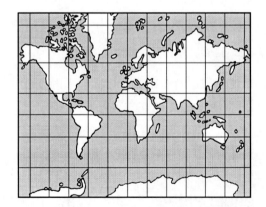

Name _____ Date _____ Class _____

Mapping Earth's Surface

Maps and Computers (pages 21–23)

Computer Mapping (page 21)

Key Concept: With computers, mapmakers can store, process, and display map data electronically.

- For hundreds of years, maps were drawn by hand. Early maps were based only on what people saw.
- Later maps were based on data from surveying. In **surveying**, distances and elevations are measured with instruments.
- Since the 1970s, computers have been used to make maps. In computer mapping, places are represented by numbers. This is called **digitizing**. The numbers are stored in a computer. The computer uses the numbers to make maps.

Answer the following questions. Use your textbook and the ideas above.

1. Read the words in the box. In each sentence below, fill in one of the words.

   | digitizing | mapping | surveying |

   a. Measuring distances and elevations with instruments is called _____.

   b. Representing places by numbers is called _____.

2. Is the following sentence true or false? Most maps today are drawn by hand. _____

Name _____ Date _____ Class _____

Mapping Earth's Surface

Sources of Map Data (pages 22–23)

Key Concept: **Computers produce maps using data from many sources, including satellites and the Global Positioning System.**

- Satellites in space collect data about Earth's surface. The satellites send the data to computers on Earth.

- The computers use the data to make pictures. The pictures are called **satellite images**.

- Satellite images show what materials cover Earth's surface. Different materials show up as different colors in the images. For example, forests are red and water is black.

- Today, some maps are based on GPS data. GPS stands for **Global Positioning System**. GPS uses satellites to find latitude, longitude, and elevation of places on Earth's surface.

Answer the following questions. Use your textbook and the ideas above.

3. Circle the letter of each sentence that is true about satellite images.
    a. Satellite images are based on GPS data.
    b. Satellite images use symbols to show features such as forests.
    c. Satellite images show what materials cover Earth's surface.

4. Circle the letter of each kind of data that you can get from the Global Positioning System.
    a. what materials cover the surface
    b. latitude
    c. longitude

Name _____ Date _____ Class _____

Mapping Earth's Surface

Topographic Maps (pages 26–30)

Mapping Earth's Topography (page 27)

Key Concept: **Mapmakers use contour lines to represent elevation, relief, and slope on topographic maps.**

- A **topographic** (tahp uh GRAF ik) **map** is a map that shows elevation, relief, and slope. Slope is how steep or flat the ground is.

- A topographic map shows elevation, relief, and slope with contour lines. A **contour line** connects points that have the same elevation.

- Every fifth contour line is called an **index contour**. Index contours are darker than other contour lines. Index contours also are labeled with the elevation.

- The **contour interval** is the change in elevation from one contour line to the next.

Answer the following questions. Use your textbook and the ideas above.

1. A map that shows elevation and relief is a(an)

   _____ map.

2. Draw a line from each term to its meaning.

Term	Meaning
contour interval	a. line connecting points that have the same elevation
contour line	b. darker line that is labeled with the elevation
index contour	c. change in elevation between contour lines

Name _____ Date _____ Class _____

Mapping Earth's Surface

Reading a Topographic Map (pages 28–29)

Key Concept: **To read a topographic map, you must familiarize yourself with the map's scale and symbols and interpret the map's contour lines.**

- Topographic maps are usually large-scale maps. Large-scale maps show a close-up view of a small area.

- Like other maps, topographic maps use symbols to show features such as rivers, swamps, highways, and airports.

- A topographic map also has contour lines. You can tell the slope of an area from the contour lines. Where contour lines are close together, the ground has a steep slope. Where contour lines are far apart, the ground has a gentle slope.

- If a contour line is a closed loop without any other contour lines inside the loop, it shows a hilltop. If the closed loop has dashes inside, it shows a hollow.

Answer the following questions. Use your textbook and the ideas above.

3. Is the following sentence true or false? Topographic maps show only elevation and relief. _____

4. Label each set of contour lines to show whether it stands for a steep slope, gentle slope, hilltop, or hollow.

  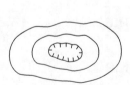 

a. _____ b. _____ c. _____ d. _____

_____   _____

Name _____ Date _____ Class _____

Mapping Earth's Surface

Uses of Topographic Maps (page 30)

Key Concept: **Topographic maps have many uses in science and engineering, business, government, and everyday life.**

- Remember, topographic maps show how steeply or gently the land slopes. Topographic maps also show where there are rivers, swamps, and other features.

- Topographic maps can be used to plan highways. The maps also can be used to decide where to build new houses, factories, and other buildings.

- A topographic map can even be used to plan a bicycle trip. The map shows where the trip would be flat or hilly.

Answer the following questions. Use your textbook and the ideas above.

5. Circle the letter of each use for a topographic map.
    a. planning a bike path that is not too hilly
    b. finding out where the ground is steep enough to build a ski slope
    c. learning how much rain a city gets each year

6. Is the following sentence true or false? Topographic maps would be useful for planning a new highway.

    _____

Weathering and Soil Formation

Rocks and Weathering (pages 38–45)

Weathering and Erosion (page 39)

Key Concept: Weathering and erosion work together continuously to wear down and carry away the rocks at Earth's surface.

- **Weathering** is the breaking down of rocks and other materials at Earth's surface. There are two kinds of weathering: mechanical weathering and chemical weathering.

- Weathering is caused by heat, cold, water, ice, and gases in the air. For example, heat and cold crack rocks into smaller pieces.

- **Erosion** (ee ROH zhun) is the movement of rock pieces and other materials on Earth's surface. Erosion is caused by wind, water, ice, and gravity. Erosion carries away the rock pieces made by weathering.

Answer the following questions. Use your textbook and the ideas above.

1. Read the words in the box. In each sentence below, fill in one of the words.

   | erosion | gravity | weathering |

   a. The breaking down of rocks and other materials at Earth's surface is called _____.

   b. The movement of rock pieces and other materials on Earth's surface is called _____.

Name _____ Date _____ Class _____

Weathering and Soil Formation

2. Fill in the blank in the concept map about kinds of weathering.

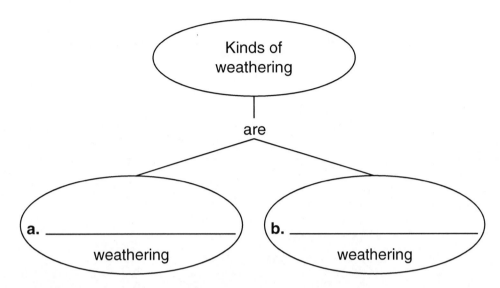

Mechanical Weathering (pages 40–41)

Key Concept: **The causes of mechanical weathering include freezing and thawing, release of pressure, plant growth, actions of animals, and abrasion.**

- In **mechanical weathering**, rock is broken into smaller pieces. But the makeup of rock does not change.

- Freezing and thawing cause **ice wedging**.

- In ice wedging, water seeps into a crack in a rock. The water freezes. Ice needs more space than water, so the ice pushes the crack apart. The ice melts. Water seeps into the deeper crack. This process keeps repeating until the rock breaks apart.

- Plant roots can grow into cracks and break apart rocks. Animals that dig in the ground can also break apart rocks.

- Rock particles can be carried by water, ice, wind, or gravity. The particles scrape rock like sandpaper scrapes wood. This scraping is called **abrasion** (uh BRAY shun).

Weathering and Soil Formation

Answer the following questions. Use your textbook and the ideas on page 19.

3. The kind of weathering that breaks rock into smaller pieces without changing the makeup of rock is _____ weathering.

4. Fill in the blanks in the cycle diagram about ice wedging. You can find the answers in the summary on page 19.

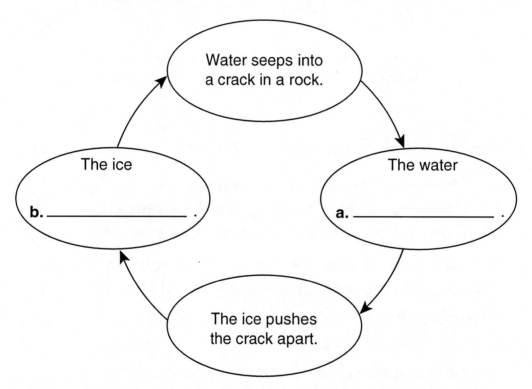

5. Circle the letter of each example of mechanical weathering.
   a. Moles dig tunnels in the ground.
   b. Wind blows sand against a rock.
   c. Plant roots grow into a crack in a rock.

Name _____ Date _____ Class _____

Weathering and Soil Formation

Chemical Weathering (pages 42–43)

Key Concept: **The causes of chemical weathering include the action of water, oxygen, carbon dioxide, living organisms, and acid rain.**

- In **chemical weathering**, the makeup of rock changes.
- Chemical weathering makes holes or soft spots in rock. This makes it easier for mechanical weathering to break rocks into smaller pieces.
- Water slowly dissolves rock.
- Some rocks contain iron. Oxygen turns iron to rust. When iron in rocks turns to rust, the rocks get soft.
- Carbon dioxide in air mixes with rainwater to make a weak acid. The acid easily dissolves some rocks.
- Plant roots also make weak acids. The acids slowly dissolve rocks around the roots.
- Acid rain is rain that contains acids because of air pollution. Acid rain quickly dissolves rocks.

Answer the following questions. Use your textbook and the ideas above.

6. Fill in the blanks in the concept map about chemical weathering.

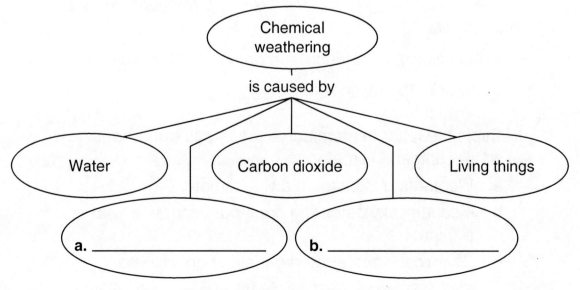

© Pearson Education, Inc., publishing as Pearson Prentice Hall. All rights reserved.

Weathering and Soil Formation

7. How does chemical weathering help mechanical weathering? Circle the letter of each correct answer.
   a. by breaking rocks into smaller pieces
   b. by making holes in rocks
   c. by making rocks softer

Rate of Weathering (pages 44–45)

Key Concept: **The most important factors that determine the rate at which weathering occurs are the type of rock and the climate.**

- The rate of weathering is how fast a rock weathers. Some kinds of rock weather faster than others.

- Certain minerals dissolve easily in water. Rocks made of these minerals weather quickly. Some rocks are full of tiny holes that water can enter. These rocks also weather quickly.

- Rocks weather more quickly in some climates than in other climates. Climate is an area's average weather.

- Both mechanical and chemical weathering are faster in a wet climate than in a dry climate. Mechanical weathering is faster in a cool climate. Chemical weathering is faster in a warm climate.

Answer the following questions. Use your textbook and the ideas above.

8. Is the following sentence true or false? All rocks weather at the same rate. _____

9. Circle the letter of each sentence that is true about weathering and climate.
   a. Weathering is faster in a wet climate.
   b. Mechanical weathering does not occur in a warm climate.
   c. Chemical weathering requires a cool climate.

Name _____ Date _____ Class _____

Weathering and Soil Formation

How Soil Forms (pages 48–54)

What Is Soil? (pages 48–49)

***Key Concept:* Soil is a mixture of rock particles, minerals, decayed organic material, water, and air.**

- **Soil** is the material on Earth's surface in which plants can grow. Soil contains pieces of rock and other materials.
- Most pieces of rock in soil come from the weathering of bedrock. **Bedrock** is a solid layer of rock under the soil.
- Pieces of rock in soil can be small or large. Plants grow best in soils that have rock pieces of different sizes.
- When dead plants and animals decay, or break down, they form **humus** (HYOO mus). Humus mixes with rock pieces to form soil.
- Humus in soil helps plants grow. Humus makes tiny spaces in soil for air and water that plants need. Humus also contains substances called minerals that plants need.

Answer the following questions. Use your textbook and the ideas above.

1. Read the words in the box. In each sentence below, fill in one of the words.

   | humus | bedrock | water | soil |

   a. The material on Earth's surface in which plants can grow is _____.

   b. The material that forms when plants and animals decay is _____.

   c. Most pieces of rock in soil come from weathering of _____.

© Pearson Education, Inc., publishing as Pearson Prentice Hall. All rights reserved.

Weathering and Soil Formation

2. Why is humus good for plants? Circle the letter of each correct answer.
   a. Humus makes spaces in soil for air and water.
   b. Humus contains minerals that plants need.
   c. Humus makes bedrock weather faster.

The Process of Soil Formation (page 50)

Key Concept: Soil forms as rock is broken down by weathering and mixes with other materials on the surface. Soil is constantly being formed wherever bedrock is exposed.

- Soil forms in layers called horizons. A **soil horizon** is a layer of soil that is different from the soil above it or below it.

- The top layer of soil is the A horizon, or topsoil. **Topsoil** is a mixture of humus and tiny rock pieces.

- Below the A horizon is the B horizon, or subsoil. **Subsoil** is made up mostly of rock pieces.

- The bottom layer of soil is the C horizon. The C horizon contains only partly weathered rock pieces.

- The C horizon forms first, as bedrock weathers. The A horizon forms next, as humus is added to rock pieces on the surface. The B horizon forms last, as smaller pieces of rock wash down from the A horizon.

Answer the following questions. Use your textbook and the ideas above.

3. Circle the letter of the correct order in which soil horizons form.
   a. A→B→C
   b. C→B→A
   c. C→A→B

Name _____ Date _____ Class _____

Weathering and Soil Formation

4. Label the soil horizons in the diagram. Use the letters A, B, and C.

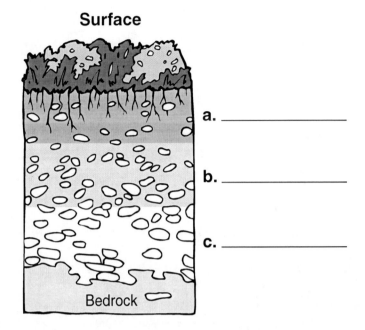

Surface

a. _____

b. _____

c. _____

Bedrock

5. Draw a line from each term to its meaning.

Term	Meaning
topsoil	a. soil that contains pieces of rock and humus
subsoil	b. soil that contains rock pieces and clay

Soil Types (page 51)

Key Concept: **Scientists classify the different types of soil into major groups based on climate, plants, and soil composition.**

- Climate affects the kind of soil in an area. For example, in a rainy climate, humus may be washed out of the soil.

- Different kinds of plants grow in different kinds of soil. For example, prairie plants such as grasses grow in a different kind of soil than forest plants such as trees.

- Soil composition is the makeup of soil. For example, the composition of soil can be rocky or sandy.

© Pearson Education, Inc., publishing as Pearson Prentice Hall. All rights reserved.

Name _____ Date _____ Class _____

Weathering and Soil Formation

- In the United States, forest soil covers most of the eastern states. Desert soil and mountain soil cover most of the western states. Prairie soil is found in between.

Answer the following questions. Use your textbook and the ideas on page 25 and above.

6. Fill in the blanks in the concept map about soil types.

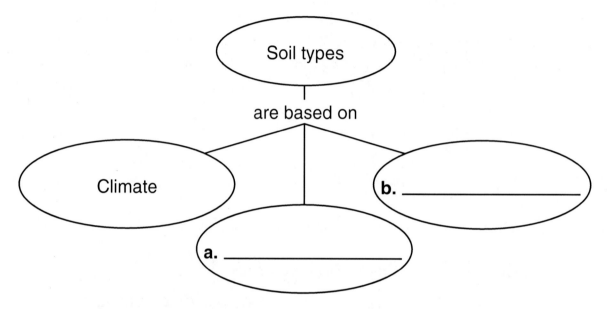

7. Label the map with the kind of soil found in each area. Use the following soil types: Forest soil, Mountain soil, Prairie soil, and Desert soil. One area has more than one kind of soil.

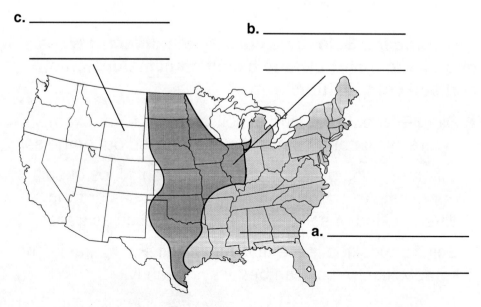

Name _____ Date _____ Class _____

Weathering and Soil Formation

Living Organisms in Soil (pages 52–54)

Key Concept: **Some soil organisms make humus, the material that makes soil fertile. Other soil organisms mix the soil and make spaces in it for air and water.**

- Living things in soil break down dead plants and animals. This process makes humus. The process is called decomposition.
- Living things that break down dead organisms are called **decomposers**. Bacteria and mushrooms are examples of decomposers.
- Earthworms and burrowing animals such as moles mix humus and air into soil.

Answer the following questions. Use your textbook and the ideas above.

8. Draw a line from each term to its meaning.

Term	Meaning
decomposer	a. process in which humus forms
decomposition	b. living thing that turns dead plants and animals into humus

9. What do earthworms and burrowing animals do to soil? Circle the letter of each correct answer.

   a. break down, or decompose, dead plants and animals
   b. mix humus into soil
   c. mix air into soil

© Pearson Education, Inc., publishing as Pearson Prentice Hall. All rights reserved.

Name _____ Date _____ Class _____

Weathering and Soil Formation

Soil Conservation (pages 56–59)

The Value of Soil (page 57)

Key Concept: Soil is one of Earth's most valuable natural resources because everything that lives on land, including humans, depends directly or indirectly on soil.

- A **natural resource** is anything in the environment that humans use.

- Plants depend directly on soil to live and grow. Humans and other animals depend on plants for food. So, humans and other animals depend indirectly on soil.

- Soil that is good for growing plants is valuable because there is not very much of it. Less than one eighth of the soil on Earth is good for farming.

Answer the following questions. Use your textbook and the ideas above.

1. Anything in the environment that humans use is called a(an) _____.

2. Circle the letter of each sentence that is true about the value of soil.
    a. Only plants depend on soil.
    b. Less than one eighth of Earth's soil is good for farming.
    c. Soil is not a natural resource.

3. Is the following sentence true or false? People do not depend on soil for anything. _____

Name _____ Date _____ Class _____

Weathering and Soil Formation

Soil Damage and Loss (pages 57–58)

Key Concept: The value of soil is reduced when soil loses its fertility and when topsoil is lost due to erosion.

- Soil fertility is a measure of how good soil is for plants. A soil with high fertility has everything plants need to grow and stay healthy.

- Soil can lose its fertility if farmers grow just one kind of plant year after year.

- When soil is bare, water and wind can carry the soil away. Plants protect soil from erosion. For example, plant roots help hold soil together.

- States such as Oklahoma used to be covered with grass. Then farmers plowed up the grass to plant crops. In the 1930s, dry weather killed the crops and turned the bare soil to dust. Wind blew away the dust.

- The area was called the **Dust Bowl**. The Dust Bowl taught people to take better care of the soil.

Answer the following questions. Use your textbook and the ideas above.

4. Circle the letter of each way that soil can become less valuable.
    a. Soil can lose its fertility.
    b. Soil can be lost because of erosion.
    c. Soil can be covered with plants.

5. Circle the letter of each sentence that is true about the Dust Bowl.
    a. The Dust Bowl included Oklahoma.
    b. In the Dust Bowl, water washed away the soil.
    c. The Dust Bowl taught people to take better care of the soil.

Name _____ Date _____ Class _____

Weathering and Soil Formation

Soil Conservation (page 59)

Key Concept: **Soil can be conserved through contour plowing, conservation plowing, and crop rotation.**

- **Soil conservation** means using soil in ways that save it. Soil conservation keeps soil fertile and prevents soil erosion.

- In **contour plowing**, farmers plow fields along curves of slopes instead of straight up and down slopes. This keeps soil from washing away in heavy rains.

- In **conservation plowing**, farmers leave dead weeds and stalks in the fields. The dead plants hold soil in place. The plants also turn into humus, which makes soil more fertile.

- In **crop rotation**, farmers grow different kinds of plants in their fields each year. Crop rotation keeps soil from losing its fertility.

Answer the following questions. Use your textbook and the ideas above.

6. Using soil in ways that save it is called _____.

7. Draw a line from each method of soil conservation to its description.

Method	Description
contour plowing	a. leaving dead plants in fields
crop rotation	b. plowing fields along curves of slopes
conservation plowing	c. growing different kinds of plants in a field each year

© Pearson Education, Inc., publishing as Pearson Prentice Hall. All rights reserved.

Name _____ Date _____ Class _____

Erosion and Deposition

Changing Earth's Surface (pages 66–69)

Wearing Down and Building Up (pages 66–67)

Key Concept: **Weathering, erosion, and deposition act together in a cycle that wears down and builds up Earth's surface.**

- **Erosion** is the movement of pieces of rock and other materials on Earth's surface. Erosion can be caused by gravity, running water, glaciers, waves, or wind.

- **Sediment** is the material moved by erosion. Sediment is made up of pieces of rock or soil or remains of living things.

- Most sediment comes from weathering. Remember, weathering is the breaking down of rock and other materials at Earth's surface.

- **Deposition** happens when sediment is dropped. Dropped sediment can build up over time and make new landforms.

Answer the following questions. Use your textbook and the ideas above.

1. Draw a line from each term to its meaning.

Term	Meaning
weathering	a. the material moved by erosion
erosion	b. the movement of pieces of rock and other materials on Earth's surface
sediment	c. the dropping of sediment
deposition	d. the breaking down of rock and other materials at Earth's surface

Erosion and Deposition

2. Circle the letter of each choice that is a cause of erosion.
   a. gravity
   b. running water
   c. weathering

Mass Movement (pages 67–69)

Key Concept: **The different types of mass movement include landslides, mudflows, slump, and creep.**

- **Mass movement** is any process that moves sediment downhill. Mass movement is caused by gravity. **Gravity** is the force that pulls everything toward Earth's center.
- Landslides happen when rocks and soil quickly slide down a steep slope.
- Mudflows happen when rocks and mud quickly slide down a steep slope.
- Slump happens when a mass of rocks and soil suddenly slides down a steep slope. Slump is different than a landslide. The material in slump moves down the slope in one large mass.
- Creep happens when rocks and soil move very slowly down a hill. Creep can happen even on gentle slopes.

Answer the following questions. Use your textbook and the ideas above.

3. Any process that moves sediment downhill is called _____.

4. Circle the letter of the cause of mass movement.
   a. rain
   b. wind
   c. gravity

Name _____ Date _____ Class _____

Erosion and Deposition

5. Fill in the blanks in the concept map about kinds of mass movement.

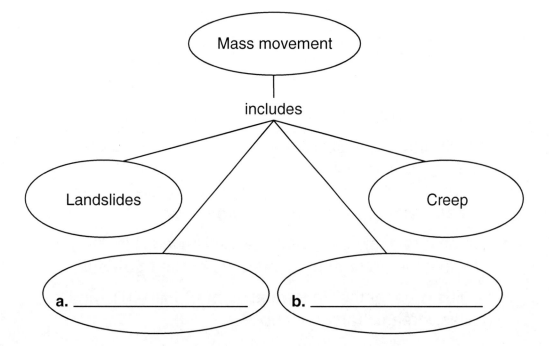

Erosion and Deposition

Water Erosion (pages 72–81)

Runoff and Erosion (pages 73–74)

Key Concept: **Moving water is the major agent of the erosion that has shaped Earth's land surface.**

- Falling raindrops can loosen and pick up soil particles.
- Rainfall that does not soak in but runs over the ground is called **runoff**. Runoff picks up more soil particles. There is more runoff if the rain is heavy or the ground is bare or steep. More runoff causes more erosion.
- Runoff forms tiny grooves in the soil called **rills**. Rills flow together to form bigger grooves called **gullies**.
- Gullies join together to form **streams**. Unlike rills and gullies, streams rarely dry up.
- Streams join together to form rivers. A **tributary** is a stream or river that flows into a bigger river.

Answer the following questions. Use your textbook and the ideas above.

1. Fill in the blanks in the flowchart showing how runoff flows into rivers.

From Runoff to Rivers

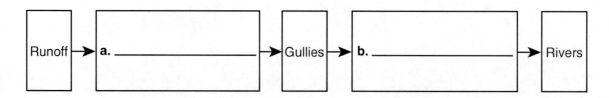

2. A stream or river that flows into a bigger river is called a(an) _____.

Name _____ Date _____ Class _____

Erosion and Deposition

Erosion by Rivers (pages 75–76)

Key Concept: **Through erosion, a river creates valleys, waterfalls, flood plains, meanders, and oxbow lakes.**

- A river on a steep slope flows quickly. The fast-moving water wears away a deep, V-shaped valley.

- A river may flow from hard rock to soft rock. The soft rock wears away faster than the hard rock. This causes a sharp drop in the riverbed, which forms a waterfall.

- A river on a gentle slope spreads out and flows slowly. The slow-moving water slowly wears away a wide, flat-bottomed valley. The valley is called a **flood plain**.

- A **meander** is a big bend in a river. A meander forms in a flood plain. It starts as a small curve and gets bigger.

- An **oxbow lake** is a meander that has been cut off from a river. An oxbow lake is curved like a meander.

Answer the following questions. Use your textbook and the ideas above.

3. Fill in the blanks in the drawing. Use the following terms: Waterfall, Meander, and Oxbow lake.

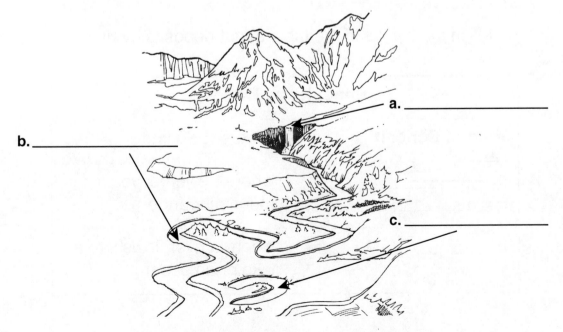

Name _____ Date _____ Class _____

Erosion and Deposition

4. Is the following sentence true or false? A river forms a flood plain when it flows over a steep slope.

   _____

Deposits by Rivers (pages 76–79)

Key Concept: Deposition creates landforms such as alluvial fans and deltas. It can also add soil to a river's flood plain.

- Rivers slow down when they leave mountains, flow into lakes or oceans, or flood their banks. When rivers slow down, they drop the sediment they are carrying. The dropped sediment is called a deposit.

- An **alluvial fan** is a deposit that forms where a river leaves a mountain range.

- A **delta** is a deposit that forms where a river flows into a lake or an ocean.

- When a river floods, it drops sediment on its flood plain. This may happen year after year. This explains why flood plain soil is usually thick and fertile.

Answer the following questions. Use your textbook and the ideas above.

5. Fill in the blanks in the table about deposits by rivers.

Deposits by Rivers	
Kind of Deposit	**Where It Forms**
a. _____	where a river leaves a mountain range
b. _____	where a river flows into a lake or an ocean

Erosion and Deposition

6. Circle the letter of the sentence that explains why a flood plain usually has thick, fertile soil.

    a. A river slows down and drops sediment when it floods its banks.

    b. A river flows faster when it flows over its flood plain.

    c. A river never flows over its flood plain, so flood plain soil is not washed away.

Groundwater Erosion (pages 80–81)

Key Concept: **Groundwater can cause erosion through a process of chemical weathering.**

- When it rains, some water sinks into the ground. Underground water is called **groundwater**.

- Groundwater mixes with carbon dioxide in soil and becomes a weak acid. Groundwater can dissolve limestone and make holes in the rock. Big holes in limestone are called caves.

- Groundwater often drips from the roof of a cave. Dissolved substances can come out of the dripping water and form deposits that look like icicles.

- When one of these deposits hangs down from the roof of a cave, it is called a **stalactite** (stuh LAK tyt).

- When one of these deposits sticks up from the floor of a cave, it is called a **stalagmite** (stuh LAG myt).

- If the roof of a cave wears away, the land over it may sink in and make a hole in the ground. The hole is called a sinkhole.

Answer the following questions. Use your textbook and the ideas above.

7. Underground water is called _____.

Name _____ Date _____ Class _____

Erosion and Deposition

8. Draw a line from each term to its meaning.

Term	Meaning
stalagmite	a. deposit that hangs down from the roof of a cave
stalactite	b. deposit that sticks up from the floor of a cave

9. When the roof of a cave wears away and the ground sinks in, it forms a(an) _____.

Name _____ Date _____ Class _____

Erosion and Deposition

The Force of Moving Water (pages 86–90)

Work and Energy (page 86)

Key Concept: **As gravity pulls water down a slope, the water's potential energy changes to kinetic energy that can do work.**

- Moving water has energy. An object has **energy** if it can do work. Moving water can run machines.
- Two kinds of energy are potential energy and kinetic energy.
- **Potential energy** is stored energy. This kind of energy is waiting to be used. Water behind a dam has potential energy.
- **Kinetic energy** is the energy of moving objects. Water moving over a dam has kinetic energy.

Answer the following questions. Use your textbook and the ideas above.

1. An object that can do work has _____.

2. Fill in the blanks in the table about kinds of energy.

Kinds of Energy	
Kind of Energy	**Description**
a. _____ energy	stored energy
b. _____ energy	energy of moving objects

Name _____ Date _____ Class _____

Erosion and Deposition

How Water Erodes (page 87)

Key Concept: **Most sediment washes or falls into a river as a result of mass movement and runoff. Other sediment erodes from the bottom or sides of the river.**

- A river erodes Earth's surface by picking up and moving sediment. Sediment can get into a river in different ways.
- A landslide can dump sediment into a river. Runoff can wash sediment into a river. A river can also get sediment by abrasion.
- In **abrasion**, sediment in the water scrapes against the bottom and sides of the river. Bits of rock are chipped away to form new sediment.
- Sediment **load** is the amount of sediment a river carries.
- Sediment moves downstream with the water. Bigger pieces of sediment roll or bounce along the bottom. Smaller pieces are lifted and carried by the water.

Answer the following question. Use your textbook and the ideas above.

3. Read the words in the box. In each sentence below, fill in one of the words.

| load | abrasion | runoff | sediment |

   a. A river erodes the surface by picking up and moving _____.

   b. How much sediment a river carries is its sediment _____.

   c. The scraping of the bottom and sides of a river by sediment is called _____.

© Pearson Education, Inc., publishing as Pearson Prentice Hall. All rights reserved.

Name _____ Date _____ Class _____

Erosion and Deposition

Erosion and Sediment Load (pages 88–90)

Key Concept: **A river's slope, volume of flow, and the shape of its streambed all affect how fast the river flows and how much sediment it can erode.**

- How much erosion a river can cause depends mainly on how much sediment the river can carry. The amount of sediment a river can carry depends on how fast the water moves and how much water there is.

- Fast-moving water can carry more sediment than slow-moving water. Fast-moving water can also carry bigger pieces of sediment.

- A big river with a lot of water can carry more sediment than a small river. A big river can also carry bigger pieces of sediment.

- Big rocks in a streambed can make water rough. Rough water wears away the streambed faster than smooth water.

- Where a river curves, water moves faster along the outside of the curve. The faster water wears away the outside bank. The water moves slower on the inside of the curve. The slower water drops sediment along the inside bank. In this way, the curve keeps getting bigger.

Answer the following questions. Use your textbook and the ideas above.

4. How much erosion a river can cause depends mainly on how much _____ the river can carry.

5. Circle the letter of each sentence that is true about erosion by rivers.

   a. A fast river causes more erosion than a slow river.

   b. A small river causes more erosion than a big river.

   c. A river with rough water causes more erosion than a river with smooth water.

© Pearson Education, Inc., publishing as Pearson Prentice Hall. All rights reserved.

Name _____ Date _____ Class _____

Erosion and Deposition

Glaciers (pages 91–95)

How Glaciers Form and Move (pages 92–93)

Key Concept: **There are two kinds of glaciers—continental glaciers and valley glaciers. Glaciers can form only in an area where more snow falls than melts. Once the depth of snow and ice reaches more than 30 to 40 meters, gravity begins to pull the glacier downhill.**

- A **glacier** is a huge chunk of ice that moves over the land. A glacier forms when snow and ice build up year after year.

- A **continental glacier** covers all or most of a continent. This kind of glacier moves very slowly in all directions.

- At times, continental glaciers have covered much of Earth's surface. These times are called **ice ages**.

- A **valley glacier** is a long, narrow glacier in a mountain valley. A valley glacier moves only down the valley. A valley glacier can move faster than a continental glacier.

Answer the following questions. Use your textbook and the ideas above.

1. A huge chunk of ice that moves over the land is a(an) _____.

2. Fill in the blanks in the Venn diagram about glaciers.

a. _____   b. _____
   Glacier   **Glacier**

   Long and narrow   Very wide

   Forms when snow and ice build up

   Moves faster   Moves slower

© Pearson Education, Inc., publishing as Pearson Prentice Hall. All rights reserved.

42

Name _____ Date _____ Class _____

Erosion and Deposition

How Glaciers Shape the Land (pages 93–95)

Key Concept: **The two processes by which glaciers erode the land are plucking and abrasion.**

- As a glacier moves, it erodes the land under it.
- The weight of a glacier can break off pieces of rock. The rock pieces stick to the glacier and become sediment. This process is called **plucking**.
- As the glacier moves, the sediment on the bottom scrapes the land. The scraping is called abrasion.
- Abrasion can make valleys wider. Abrasion can also scrape away mountainsides. This leaves a sharp mountain peak called a horn.

Answer the following questions. Use your textbook and the ideas above.

3. Draw a line from each term to its meaning.

Term	Meaning
plucking	a. process in which sediment scrapes the land
abrasion	b. process in which rocks are picked up by glaciers

4. Is the following sentence true or false? Glaciers can make valleys wider and scrape away mountain sides.

    _____

Key Concept: **When a glacier melts, it deposits the sediment it eroded from the land, creating various landforms.**

- Wherever a glacier melts, it drops its sediment. Sediment dropped by a glacier is called **till**. Till makes many different landforms.

Erosion and Deposition

- A **moraine** is a ridge or mound that forms where till is dropped along the edge of a glacier.
- Sometimes a glacier drops a big chunk of ice instead of rock or soil. When the ice melts, it leaves a low spot in the ground called a **kettle**.

Answer the following questions. Use your textbook and the ideas on page 43 and above.

5. The sediment dropped by a glacier is called _____.

6. Fill in the blanks in the table about landforms from glaciers.

Landforms from Glaciers	
Landform	**Description**
Horn	sharp mountain peak formed by abrasion
a. _____	low spot in the ground formed by a big chunk of ice
b. _____	ridge or mound formed by till at the edge of a glacier

Name _____ Date _____ Class _____

Erosion and Deposition

Waves (pages 96–100)

How Waves Form (page 96)

Key Concept: **The energy in waves comes from wind that blows across the water's surface.**

- When ocean wind touches ocean water, energy passes from the wind to the water. This energy causes waves. The waves carry the energy across the ocean.
- Where the ocean is deep, waves affect only the surface of the water.
- Close to shore, the water is shallow. There, waves drag on the bottom and crash against the shore.

Answer the following questions. Use your textbook and the ideas above.

1. Circle the letter of each sentence that is true about ocean waves.
    a. Ocean waves cause ocean winds.
    b. Ocean waves carry energy across the ocean.
    c. Ocean waves affect only the surface of deep water.

2. How do ocean waves change close to shore? Circle the letter of the correct answer.
    a. The waves move higher in the water.
    b. The waves drag on the bottom.
    c. The waves affect only the water's surface.

Name _____ Date _____ Class _____

Erosion and Deposition

Erosion by Waves (pages 97–98)

***Key Concept:* Waves shape the coast through erosion by breaking down rock and transporting sand and other sediment.**

- Waves are the major cause of erosion along coasts. When waves hit the shore, the force of the water can crack rocks. Over time, the rocks break into smaller pieces and wash away.

- Close to shore, waves pick up sediment from the bottom. When the waves hit rocks on shore, the sediment wears away the rocks by abrasion.

- Some rock on shore may be harder than the rock around it. The harder rock wears away slower and forms a headland. A **headland** is part of a shore that sticks out into the ocean.

- Waves can wear away the bottoms of cliffs along the shore. Waves can also wear away holes in cliffs and form caves.

Answer the following question. Use your textbook and the ideas above.

3. Read the words in the box. In each sentence below, fill in one of the words.

| cliff | abrasion | headland | waves |

a. A part of a shore that sticks out into the ocean is called a(an) _____.

b. The major cause of erosion along coasts is _____.

c. Waves that carry sediment cause _____.

Name _____ Date _____ Class _____

Erosion and Deposition

Deposits by Waves (pages 99–100)

Key Concept: **Waves shape a coast when they deposit sediment, forming coastal features such as beaches, spits, and barrier beaches.**

- When waves slow down at a coast, they drop sediment. The sediment can build up to make different landforms.
- A **beach** is an area of sediment at the edge of the water. The sediment on a beach is usually sand.
- If waves hit a beach at an angle, they can carry sand down the beach. This is called **longshore drift**.
- If a headland stops longshore drift, the sand piles up and forms a spit. A **spit** is a beach that sticks out into the water like a finger.
- Sometimes waves drop sand in a long ridge parallel to shore. The ridge of sand is called a sandbar. If the sand builds up above the surface of the water, it forms a long, narrow island parallel to the shore. This kind of island is called a barrier beach.

Answer the following question. Use your textbook and the ideas above.

4. Draw a line from each term to its meaning.

Term	Meaning
barrier beach	a. beach that sticks out into the water like a finger
spit	b. long ridge of sand parallel to the shore
longshore drift	c. movement of sand down a beach by waves
sandbar	d. long, narrow island parallel to the shore

Name _____ Date _____ Class _____

Erosion and Deposition

Wind (pages 101–103)

How Wind Causes Erosion (pages 101–102)

Key Concept: **Wind causes erosion by deflation and abrasion.**

- Deflation is the main way that wind causes erosion. **Deflation** is the process by which wind picks up sediment from the surface. The stronger the wind, the bigger the pieces of sediment the wind can pick up.

- Wind may carry away all the sediment in a desert and leave behind only rocks. The rocky surface that is left is called desert pavement.

- Sediment carried by wind causes abrasion. The blowing sediment scrubs and polishes rock.

Answer the following questions. Use your textbook and the ideas above.

1. The process by which wind picks up sediment from the surface is called _____.

2. Fill in the blanks in the concept map about how wind causes erosion.

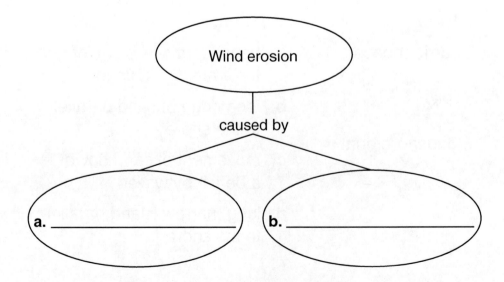

Name _____ Date _____ Class _____

Erosion and Deposition

Wind Deposition (page 103)

Key Concept: **Wind erosion and deposition may form sand dunes and loess deposits.**

- Wind drops the sediment it is carrying when a wall or other barrier slows the wind. The sediment may form sand dunes or loess deposits.

- **Sand dunes** are ridges or mounds that form when the wind drops sand. Sand dunes can be small or large. Wind may slowly move sand dunes across the ground.

- **Loess** (LES) is tiny pieces of sediment that are dropped by the wind. Loess helps make soil fertile. There are big loess deposits in states such as Nebraska and Iowa.

Answer the following questions. Use your textbook and the ideas above.

3. Is the following sentence true or false? Wind drops the sediment it is carrying when the wind slows down. _____

4. Fill in the blanks in the Venn diagram to show which circle describes a sand dune and which circle describes a loess deposit.

a. _____   b. _____

_____   _____

| Forms if sediment is sand | Forms when wind drops sediment | Forms if sediment is tiny pieces |

Name _____ Date _____ Class _____

A Trip Through Geologic Time

Fossils (pages 110–116)

How a Fossil Forms (pages 110–113)

Key Concept: Most fossils form when living things die and are buried by sediments. The sediments slowly harden into rock and preserve the shapes of the organisms.

- **Fossils** are remains of organisms that died long ago. An organism is any kind living thing.
- Fossils are usually found in **sedimentary rock**. This kind of rock forms when sediment builds up over time.
- Sedimentary rock usually forms in shallow water. So most organisms that turn into fossils once lived in or near shallow water.
- Suppose an animal dies and sinks into shallow water. Sediment slowly covers the dead animal and turns to rock. Part of the animal may also turn to rock and become a fossil.

Answer the following questions. Use your textbook and the ideas above.

1. Remains of organisms that died long ago are called _____.

2. Circle the letter of each sentence that is true about how most fossils form.
    a. Most fossils form when water washes away sediment from dead organisms.
    b. Most fossils form from organisms that once lived in or near shallow water.
    c. Most fossils form when dead organisms are buried by sediment.

Name _____ Date _____ Class _____

A Trip Through Geologic Time

Key Concept: **Fossils found in rock include molds and casts, petrified fossils, carbon films, and trace fossils. Other fossils form when the remains of organisms are preserved in substances such as tar, amber, or ice.**

- A **mold** is a hollow area in a rock in the shape of an organism. A mold forms when sediment buries a hard part of a dead organism. The hard part later breaks down and leaves a mold.

- A **cast** is a copy of an organism in rock. A cast forms when sediment fills a mold and turns to rock.

- **Petrified fossils** are dead organisms that have turned to stone. Water soaks into dead organisms. Minerals in the water harden and turn into stone.

- All organisms contain carbon. When a dead organism breaks down in rock, it may leave behind a thin **carbon film** on the rock. The film is like a picture of the organism.

- **Trace fossils** show how ancient organisms behaved. Trace fossils include fossil footprints and burrows.

- Sometimes organisms are trapped in something sticky that keeps them from breaking down. For example, insects may be trapped in tree sap. The sap hardens around the insect and forms a clear solid called amber.

Answer the following question. Use your textbook and the ideas above.

3. Draw a line from each kind of fossil to its description.

Kind of Fossil	**Description**
carbon film	a. hollow area in rock in the shape of an organism
mold	
	b. solid copy of an organism in rock
trace fossil	
	c. organism that has turned to stone
petrified fossil	d. thin layer of carbon on rock
cast	e. preserved trace such as a footprint

© Pearson Education, Inc., publishing as Pearson Prentice Hall. All rights reserved.

Name _____ Date _____ Class _____

A Trip Through Geologic Time

Change Over Time (pages 114–116)

Key Concept: The fossil record provides evidence about the history of life and past environments on Earth. The fossil record also shows that different groups of organisms have changed over time.

- Scientists collect fossils from all over the world. All the fossils together make up the fossil record. The fossil record shows what past life forms were like.

- The fossil record also shows what past environments were like. For example, fossils of swamp creatures have been found in areas that are now dry. The fossils show that the areas used to be much wetter.

- The fossil record shows that organisms have changed slowly over time. For example, the fossil record shows that elephants used to have shorter trunks.

- This change in elephants is an example of evolution. **Evolution** is gradual change in living things that happens over a long period of time.

- The fossil record shows that all kinds of organisms have changed. The fossil record also shows that many kinds of organisms have died out, or gone **extinct**.

Answer the following questions. Use your textbook and the ideas above.

4. All the fossils that scientists have found make up the _____.

5. What have scientists learned from the fossil record? Circle the letter of each correct choice.
   a. what past environments were like
   b. what past life forms were like
   c. how organisms have changed over time

Name _____ Date _____ Class _____

A Trip Through Geologic Time

The Relative Age of Rocks

(pages 117–121)

The Position of Rock Layers (page 118)

Key Concept: **According to the law of superposition, in horizontal sedimentary rock layers the oldest layer is at the bottom. Each higher layer is younger than the layers below it.**

- To understand how life has changed, scientists must know how old fossils are. Scientists can tell how old fossils are from the rocks where the fossils are found.

- Remember, fossils are found in sedimentary rocks. This kind of rock forms when sediment builds up over time.

- In sedimentary rock, lower rock layers are older than upper rock layers. So fossils found in lower rock layers are older than fossils found in upper rock layers.

Answer the following question. Use your textbook and the ideas above.

4. Use the diagram below to answer the questions.

   a. Which rock layer is youngest? _____

   b. Which rock layer is oldest? _____

   c. Which fossil is older? _____

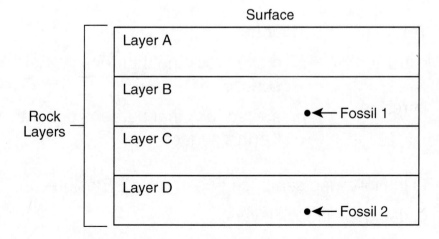

© Pearson Education, Inc., publishing as Pearson Prentice Hall. All rights reserved.

Name _____ Date _____ Class _____

A Trip Through Geologic Time

Determining Relative Age (pages 119–120)

Key Concept: **To determine relative age, geologists also study extrusions and intrusions of igneous rock, faults, and gaps in the geologic record.**

- Sedimentary rock layers do not always line up neatly. Positions of rock layers may change after the rocks form. This can happen in different ways.

- Melted rock can harden and form new rock on top or inside of sedimentary rock. New rock that forms on top of sedimentary rock is called an **extrusion**. New rock that forms inside of sedimentary rock is called an **intrusion**.

- At a fault, rock layers may move so they no longer line up. A **fault** is a break in rock where rocks can move.

- New rock layers can be worn away by erosion before they are covered by sediment. This makes a time gap in the rock layers. Younger rock layers are directly on top of very old rock layers.

Answer the following questions. Use your textbook and the ideas above.

2. A break in rock where rocks can move is a(an) _____.

3. Draw a line from each term to its meaning.

Term	Meaning
extrusion	a. melted rock that hardens on Earth's surface
intrusion	b. melted rock that hardens beneath Earth's surface

4. Is the following sentence true or false? Erosion can cause gaps in rock layers. _____

Name _____ Date _____ Class _____

A Trip Through Geologic Time

Using Fossils to Date Rocks (pages 120–121)

***Key Concept:* Index fossils are useful because they tell the relative ages of the rock layers in which they occur.**

- The rock layers in different places can be hard to match up. It can be hard to tell which layers are older and which layers are younger.

- Index fossils help scientists match rock layers in different places. An **index fossil** is a fossil of an organism that lived over a wide area and existed for just a short period of time.

- Two rock layers in different places that contain the same index fossil are about the same age.

Answer the following question. Use your textbook and the ideas above.

5. The diagram below shows rock layers and fossils from two different places, A and B. Use the diagram to answer the questions.

   a. Which fossil could be an index fossil? _____

   b. Use this index fossil to find the rock layer in place B that matches rock layer 2 in place A. _____

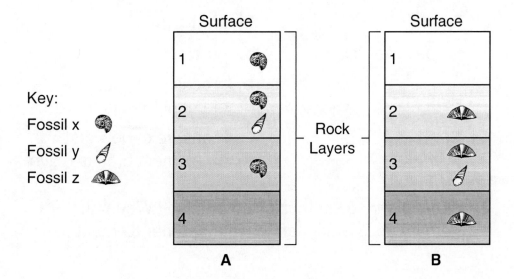

© Pearson Education, Inc., publishing as Pearson Prentice Hall. All rights reserved.

55

Name _____ Date _____ Class _____

A Trip Through Geologic Time

Radioactive Dating (pages 123–126)

Radioactive Decay (page 124)

Key Concept: **During radioactive decay, the atoms of one element break down to form atoms of another element.**

- Everything is made up of one or more pure substances. These pure substances are called **elements**.

- Some elements break down, or decay. When an element decays, it changes into another kind of element. The process is called **radioactive decay**.

- Elements that decay are called radioactive elements. Potassium-40 is an example. Potassium-40 decays into argon-40.

- How fast an element decays is given by its half-life. The **half-life** is the time it takes for half of a sample of an element to decay. For example, the half-life of potassium-40 is 1.3 billion years.

Answer the following questions. Use your textbook and the ideas above.

1. Draw a line from each term to its meaning.

Term	Meaning
radioactive decay	**a.** pure substance
element	**b.** process in which an element breaks down
half-life	**c.** measure of how fast an element breaks down

2. Is the following sentence true or false? When an element decays, it changes into another element.

   _____

Name _____ Date _____ Class _____

A Trip Through Geologic Time

Determining Absolute Ages (pages 125–126)

Key Concept: **Geologists use radioactive dating to determine the absolute ages of rocks.**

- Scientists test rocks to measure how much radioactive decay has happened. The more decay that has happened, the older the rocks is.

- This method of dating rocks is called radioactive dating. Using this method, scientists can give rocks a rough age in years. When age is given in years, it is called absolute age.

- Suppose that half of the potassium-40 in a rock has decayed to argon-40. The half-life of potassium-40 is 1.3 billion years, so the rock is about 1.3 billion years old.

- Radioactive dating works well for igneous rocks. But this kind of dating does not work well for sedimentary rocks. This is because sedimentary rocks are made of rock particles of different ages.

Answer the following questions. Use your textbook and the ideas above.

3. The method of dating rocks that gives rock a rough age in years is called _____.

4. Circle the letter of each sentence that is true about radioactive dating.
    a. Radioactive dating is based on how much radioactive decay has happened.
    b. Radioactive dating gives rocks an absolute age.
    c. Radioactive dating works well for sedimentary rock.

A Trip Through Geologic Time

5. The half-life of carbon-14 is 5,730 years. If half of the carbon-14 in a sample has decayed, how old is the sample? Circle the letter of the correct answer.

    a. 2,865 years old

    b. 5,730 years old

    c. 11,460 years old

Name _____ Date _____ Class _____

A Trip Through Geologic Time

The Geologic Time Scale
(pages 127–129)

The Geologic Time Scale (pages 127–128)

Key Concept: **Because the time span of Earth's past is so great, geologists use the geologic time scale to show Earth's history.**

- Earth has a very long history. Years and centuries are not very helpful for such a long history. So scientists use the geologic time scale for Earth's history.

- The **geologic time scale** is a record of how Earth and its life forms have changed through time. For example, the scale shows when life first appeared on Earth.

- In the geologic time scale, time is divided into bigger blocks than years or centuries. The scale begins when Earth formed 4.6 billion years ago and goes to the present.

Answer the following questions. Use your textbook and the ideas above.

1. The record of how Earth and its life forms have changed through time is the _____.

2. When does the geologic time scale begin? Circle the letter of the correct answer.
    a. 4 billion years ago
    b. 4.6 billion years ago
    c. 544 million years ago

3. Is the following sentence true or false? The geologic time scale divides time into years and centuries.
   _____

© Pearson Education, Inc., publishing as Pearson Prentice Hall. All rights reserved.

Name _____ Date _____ Class _____

A Trip Through Geologic Time

Divisions of Geologic Time (page 129)

Key Concept: After Precambrian Time, the basic units of the geologic time scale are eras and periods.

- The geologic time scale begins with a very long block of time called **Precambrian** (pree KAM bree un) **Time**. Precambrian Time goes from 4.6 billion to 544 million years ago. It covers most of Earth's history.

- The rest of the geologic time scale is divided into three major blocks of time called **eras**. The eras are the Paleozoic, Mesozoic, and Cenozoic eras.

- Each era is divided into shorter blocks of time called **periods**. For example, the Paleozoic Era is divided into six periods.

Answer the following questions. Use your textbook and the ideas above.

4. Fill in the blanks in the diagram of the geologic time scale.

Geologic Time Scale

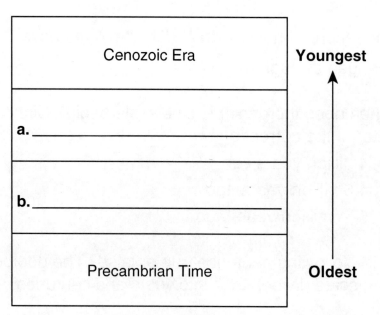

Name _____ Date _____ Class _____

A Trip Through Geologic Time

5. Which part of the geologic time scale is the longest? Circle the letter of the correct answer.
   a. Precambrian Time
   b. Paleozoic Era
   c. Cenozoic Era

6. Is the following sentence true or false? Each era of the geologic time scale is part of a longer block of time called a period. _____

Name _____ Date _____ Class _____

A Trip Through Geologic Time

Early Earth (pages 130–133)

The Planet Forms (pages 130–131)

Key Concept: **Scientists hypothesize that Earth formed at the same time as the other planets and the sun, roughly 4.6 billion years ago.**

- Rocks from the moon are known to be 4.6 billion years old. Scientists think that Earth and the moon are the same age. So Earth must also be 4.6 billion years old.

- Scientists think that Earth began as a ball of dust, rock, and ice in space. Gravity pulled these materials together, and Earth got bigger.

- As Earth got bigger, its gravity got stronger. Earth's gravity pulled more rocks toward Earth. The rocks hit Earth and gave the planet energy.

- Energy from the rocks made Earth so hot that it melted. But the surface layers later lost heat to space and got hard again.

Answer the following question. Use your textbook and the ideas above.

1. Fill in the blanks in the flowchart about how Earth formed.

How Earth Formed

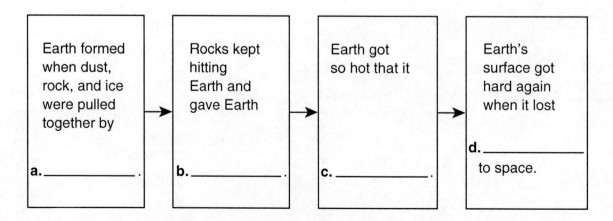

Name _____ Date _____ Class _____

A Trip Through Geologic Time

Earth's Surface Forms (page 132)

Key Concept: During the first several hundred million years of Precambrian Time, an atmosphere, oceans, and continents began to form.

- Earth slowly developed an atmosphere. This early atmosphere was made up mostly of the gases carbon dioxide, nitrogen, and water vapor.
- At first, Earth's surface was too hot for liquid water. All the water was in the form of water vapor.
- As Earth's surface cooled, liquid water formed. The water fell as rain.
- Rain slowly wore away Earth's rocky surface. Rain also collected on the surface and formed oceans.
- Continents slowly formed on Earth's surface. The continents began to move over the surface. As the continents moved, new continents formed and old continents disappeared.

Answer the following questions. Use your textbook and the ideas above.

2. Earth's early atmosphere was made up mostly of carbon dioxide, nitrogen, and _____.

3. Why was there no liquid water on early Earth? Circle the letter of the correct answer.
    a. The surface was too hot for liquid water.
    b. The planet was too dry for water to form.
    c. Earth did not yet have an atmosphere.

4. Is the following sentence true or false? Once the continents formed, they never changed.

    _____

© Pearson Education, Inc., publishing as Pearson Prentice Hall. All rights reserved.

Name _____ Date _____ Class _____

A Trip Through Geologic Time

Life Develops (page 133)

Key Concept: **Scientists have found fossils of single-celled organisms in rocks that formed about 3.5 billion years ago. These earliest life forms were probably similar to present-day bacteria.**

- The earliest forms of life on Earth lived in water. These early life forms were tiny and very simple. They slowly evolved into other forms of life.

- About 2.5 billion years ago, many organisms began using energy from the sun to make food. This way of making food is called photosynthesis.

- Oxygen is given off during photosynthesis. The oxygen collected in Earth's early atmosphere.

- Some of the oxygen turned to ozone. Ozone protects Earth's surface from the sun's rays. With ozone to protect them, organisms could live on land for the first time.

Answer the following questions. Use your textbook and the ideas above.

5. Is the following sentence true or false? There have been organisms living on land for 3.5 billion years.

   _____

6. How did photosynthesis change Earth? Circle the letter of the correct answer.

   a. Photosynthesis allowed organisms to live in the water.

   b. Photosynthesis added oxygen to Earth's early atmosphere.

   c. Photosynthesis destroyed ozone in Earth's atmosphere.

Name _____ Date _____ Class _____

A Trip Through Geologic Time

Eras of Earth's History (pages 134–145)

The Paleozoic Era (pages 135–141)

Key Concept: At the beginning of the Paleozoic Era, a great number of different kinds of organisms evolved.

- The Paleozoic (pay lee uh ZOH ik) Era is the first era after Precambrian Time. This era lasted from 544 million to 245 million years ago. The era has six periods.

- The Cambrian Period is the first period of the Paleozoic Era. In the Cambrian Period, shallow seas covered most of Earth. All organisms lived in water.

- During the Cambrian Period, there was an "explosion" of new life forms. For example, for the first time many organisms had parts such as shells.

- All animals in the Cambrian Period were invertebrates. An **invertebrate** does not have a backbone.

Answer the following question. Use your textbook and the ideas above.

1. Fill in the blanks in the concept map about life forms in the Cambrian Period.

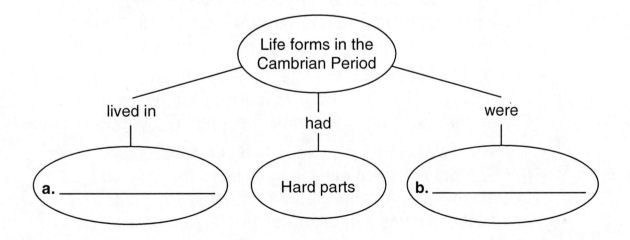

Name _____ Date _____ Class _____

A Trip Through Geologic Time

Key Concept: **During the Ordovician Period, jawless fishes evolved. Jawless fishes were the first vertebrates.**

- The Ordovician (awr duh VISH ee un) Period is the second period of the Paleozoic Era. In this period, shallow seas still covered most of Earth.

- During the Ordovician Period, the first vertebrates appeared. A **vertebrate** is an animal with a backbone. The earliest vertebrates were jawless fishes.

Answer the following questions. Use your textbook and the ideas above.

2. A major new kind of life that appeared during the Ordovician Period was _____.

3. Is the following sentence true or false? The earliest vertebrates were insects. _____

Key Concept: **During the Silurian Period, plants started living on land. During the Devonian Period, animals began to invade the land.**

- The Silurian (sih LOOR ee un) Period is the third period of the Paleozoic Era.

- During the Silurian Period, organisms lived on land for the first time. The first land organisms were plants. The first insects also appeared during this period.

- The Devonian Period is the fourth period of the Paleozoic Era. The Devonian Period is called the Age of Fishes. Fish became very common during this period.

- The first land animals also appeared in the Devonian Period. Some of these early land animals soon evolved into amphibians. An **amphibian** (am FIB ee un) is an animal that spends part of its life in water and part on land. Frogs are amphibians.

© Pearson Education, Inc., publishing as Pearson Prentice Hall. All rights reserved.

A Trip Through Geologic Time

Answer the following question. Use your textbook and the ideas on page 66.

4. Fill in the blanks in the table about events in the middle Paleozoic Era.

Events in the Middle Paleozoic Era	
Period	**Event**
a. _____	first land plants appeared
b. _____	first land animals appeared

Key Concept: During the rest of the Paleozoic Era, life expanded over Earth's continents.

- The Carboniferous Period is the fifth period of the Paleozoic Era. During this period, the climate was warm and wet. There were huge, swampy forests.

- The first reptiles appeared during the Carboniferous Period. **Reptiles** have scaly skin and lay eggs with tough, leathery shells. Lizards are reptiles.

- The first insects with wings also appeared during the Carboniferous Period.

Answer the following questions. Use your textbook and the ideas above.

5. Is the following sentence true or false? Climates were cold and dry during the Carboniferous Period.

_____

6. Which kinds of life appeared for the first time during the Carboniferous Period? Circle the letter of each correct choice.

    a. insects with wings   **b.** amphibians   **c.** reptiles

Name _____ Date _____ Class _____

A Trip Through Geologic Time

Key Concept: **During the Permian Period, about 260 million years ago, many organisms went extinct. This mass extinction affected both plants and animals, on land and in the seas. During the Permian Period, Earth's continents moved together to form a great landmass, or supercontinent, called Pangaea.**

- The last period of the Paleozoic Era is the Permian Period. Reptiles were the main land animals in this period.

- During the Permian Period, many kinds of organisms died out. When many kinds of organisms die out at the same time, it is called a **mass extinction**.

- Scientists are not sure what caused this mass extinction. But a change in climate was probably one cause.

- During the Permian Period, all of the continents moved together, so there was just one huge continent. Scientists call this huge continent Pangaea (pan JEE uh).

- As Pangaea formed, there were major changes in climate. Areas that had been warm and wet became cold and dry. Many organisms could not live in the new climate. These organisms went extinct.

Answer the following questions. Use your textbook and the ideas above.

7. What do scientists think caused the mass extinction in the Permian Period? Circle the letter of the correct answer.

    a. Many organisms could not live in the new climate.
    b. Humans appeared and killed many animals.
    c. The land was becoming too crowded.

A Trip Through Geologic Time

8. Read the words in the box. In each sentence below, fill in one of the words. The sentences are about the map. The map shows what scientists think Earth looked like 260 million years ago.

| Permian   climate   extinction   Pangaea |

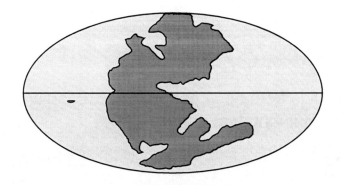

a. The name of the single, huge continent shown on the map is _____.

b. This huge continent formed during the _____ Period.

c. As this continent formed, there were major changes in _____.

Mesozoic Era (pages 142–143)

Key Concept: **Reptiles were so successful during the Mesozoic Era that this time is often called the Age of Reptiles.**

- The Mesozoic (mez uh ZOH ik) Era is the second era of the geologic time scale. This era lasted from 245 million to 66 million years ago. The era has three periods.

- The first period of the Mesozoic Era is the Triassic (try AS ik) Period. During this period, the first dinosaurs and mammals appeared. Dinosaurs were reptiles. **Mammals** are warm-blooded vertebrates that feed their young milk.

Name _____ Date _____ Class _____

A Trip Through Geologic Time

- The second period of the Mesozoic Era is the Jurassic (joo RAS ik) Period. During this period, dinosaurs became the main kind of land animals. The first birds also appeared in this period.

- The third period of the Mesozoic Era is the Cretaceous (krih TAY shus) Period. During this period, plants with flowers appeared. Reptiles were still the main vertebrates.

Answer the following question. Use your textbook and the ideas on page 69 and above.

9. Draw a line from each period to the organisms that appeared during that period.

Period	Organisms That Appeared
Triassic Period	a. plants with flowers
Jurassic Period	b. birds
Cretaceous Period	c. dinosaurs and mammals

Key Concept: At the close of the Cretaceous Period, about 65 million years ago, another mass extinction occurred. Scientists hypothesize that this mass extinction occurred when an object from space struck Earth.

- A second mass extinction happened at the end of the Mesozoic Era. Most scientists think that this mass extinction was caused by a chunk of space rock, called an asteroid.

- Scientists think the asteroid crashed into Earth. The crash caused dust and clouds that blocked out sunlight for years. Without sunlight, many organisms died out, including all of the dinosaurs.

- Some scientists think that an asteroid crash was not the only cause of this mass extinction. They think that ashes from many volcanoes were another cause.

A Trip Through Geologic Time

Answer the following question. Use your textbook and the ideas on page 70.

10. Circle the letter of each sentence that is true about the mass extinction at the end of the Mesozoic Era.

    a. Most scientists think that an asteroid caused it.

    b. Organisms went extinct because of floods.

    c. Mammals went extinct then.

The Cenozoic Era (pages 144–145)

Key Concept: **The extinction of dinosaurs created an opportunity for mammals. During the Cenozoic Era, mammals evolved to live in many different environments—on land, in water, and even in the air.**

- The Cenozoic (sen uh ZOH ik) Era is the third era of the geologic time scale. This era began 66 million years ago and goes to the present. The era is often called the Age of Mammals. The era has two periods.

- The first period of the Cenozoic Era is the Tertiary Period. This period lasted until 1.8 million years ago.

- During the Tertiary Period, climates were mild. Many new kinds of mammals appeared. Some were very large.

Answer the following questions. Use your textbook and the ideas above.

11. The third era of the geologic time scale is the

    _____.

12. Why were so many mammals able to evolve in the Cenozoic Era? Circle the letter of the correct answer.

    a. Dinosaurs showed mammals how to survive.

    b. Dinosaurs had gone extinct.

    c. Mammals hunted dinosaurs for food.

A Trip Through Geologic Time

Key Concept: *Earth's climate cooled, causing a series of ice ages during the Quaternary Period.*

- The second period of the Cenozoic Era is the Quaternary Period. This period began 1.8 million years ago. We are still in the Quaternary Period.

- During this period, the climate got colder. At times, glaciers covered much of the land. These times are called ice ages.

- Mammals, flowering plants, and insects were the main life forms in the Quaternary Period.

- Modern humans appeared late in the Quaternary Period, around 100,000 years ago.

Answer the following questions. Use your textbook and the ideas above.

13. Which period of the Cenozoic Era are we still in?
    a. Tertiary Period
    b. Quaternary Period
    c. Modern Period

14. Fill in the blanks in the concept map about the main life forms in the Quaternary Period.

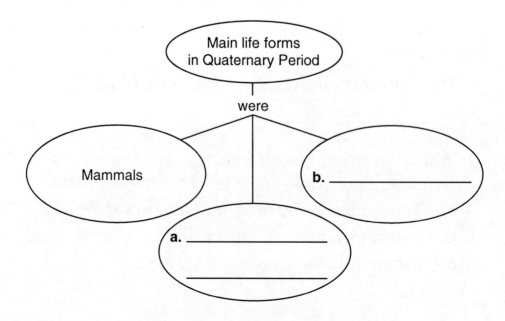